LIGHTNING BOLT BOOKS™

T0120408

Look Inside a Fire Truck

How It Works

Percy Leed

Lerner Publications ◆ Minneapolis

Lerner Publications Company
An imprint of Lerner Publishing Group, Inc.
241 First Avenue North
Minneapolis, MN 55401 USA

For reading levels and more information, look up this title at www.lernerbooks.com.

Main body text set in Billy Infant Regular. Typeface provided by SparkType.

Editor: Annie Zheng **Designer:** Martha Kranes **Photo Editor:** Nicole Berglund

Library of Congress Cataloging-in-Publication Data

Names: Leed, Percy, 1968- author.
Title: Look inside a fire truck : how it works / Percy Leed.
Description: Minneapolis : Lerner Publications, [2024] | Series: Lightning bolt books. Under the hood | Includes bibliographical references and index. | Audience: Ages 6-9 | Audience: Grades 2-3 | Summary: "Wildfires, rescue, and more! Fire trucks are responsible for saving lives and nature. Emerging readers will enjoy learning about different kinds of fire trucks and how they work"— Provided by publisher.
Identifiers: LCCN 2023013044 (print) | LCCN 2023013045 (ebook) | ISBN 9798765608470 (lib. bdg.) | ISBN 9798765624395 (pbk.) | ISBN 9798765615744 (epub)
Subjects: LCSH: Fire engines—Juvenile literature. | BISAC: JUVENILE NONFICTION / Transportation / Cars & Trucks
Classification: LCC TH9372 .L445 2024 (print) | LCC TH9372 (ebook) | DDC 628.9/259—dc23/eng/20230322

LC record available at https://lccn.loc.gov/2023013044
LC ebook record available at https://lccn.loc.gov/2023013045

Manufactured in the United States of America
1-1009613-51501-6/6/2023

Table of Contents

Racing to the Fire!

Lights flash. Sirens blare. Someone has dialed 911 to report a fire. A fire truck speeds to the scene.

Firefighters drive and use fire trucks in emergencies.

Fire trucks are vehicles that carry people and equipment to fight fires. They help save lives, buildings, and nature from fires!

Types of Fire Trucks

There are different kinds of fire trucks. The best known is the pumper truck. These trucks carry water tanks.

A firefighter starts the truck's pump by flipping a switch. This opens a valve and lets water from a tank flow into the pump.

Water goes through the pump and shoots out through a hose.

Ladder trucks are another main kind of fire truck. Ladders on these trucks help firefighters reach fires in tall buildings.

Firefighters use ladders to rescue victims trapped inside buildings.

A firefighter can make the ladder longer by using a joystick. This brings firefighters closer to fires on higher floors.

Wildfires can grow large and cause a lot of damage.

Brush trucks are fire trucks that respond to wildfires. Wildfires happen when fire spreads quickly over plant life, such as in a forest.

Brush trucks are also called wildland trucks.

Brush trucks use a pump-and-roll technique to fight wildfires. They drive and keep the valve open between the pump and water tank. Then a firefighter uses a hose to spray water on the fire.

On the Road

Fire trucks use powerful diesel engines to carry heavy loads. These engines change diesel fuel into energy that moves the truck.

Pistons are sliding pieces that go up and down.

Pistons move inside the engine. Each piston is in a tube. A piston moves up and down to squeeze air. Squeezing air makes it hot.

Engines make fire trucks move.

Fuel is sprayed on the hot air. A spark plug ignites the fuel, and the explosion pushes the piston down. The movement of all the pistons turns a crankshaft. This makes the wheels turn.

Most fire trucks use the same tires as semitrucks. Some have four tires. Larger fire trucks have six or eight tires.

Fire truck tires

Toolbox on Wheels

Compartments in fire trucks hold tools for fighting fires. Some compartments hold extra hoses.

Nozzles can also shoot foam.

Compartments can also store nozzles. Some nozzles spray a hard stream of water. Others spray mist.

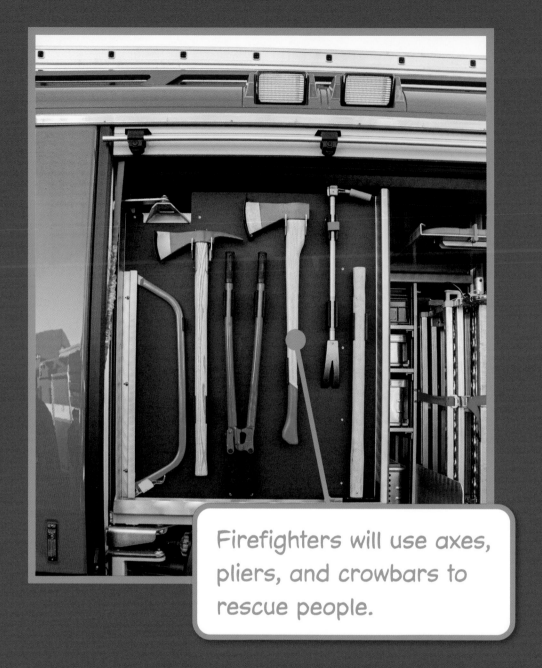

Firefighters will use axes, pliers, and crowbars to rescue people.

Firefighters rescue people trapped in cars and buildings. They use tools to cut through cars and walls.

Fire trucks carry equipment to help sick people. They carry oxygen tanks to help people who have breathed in too much smoke. If there's an emergency, fire trucks are ready!

Oxygen tanks hold clean air.

Fire Truck Diagram

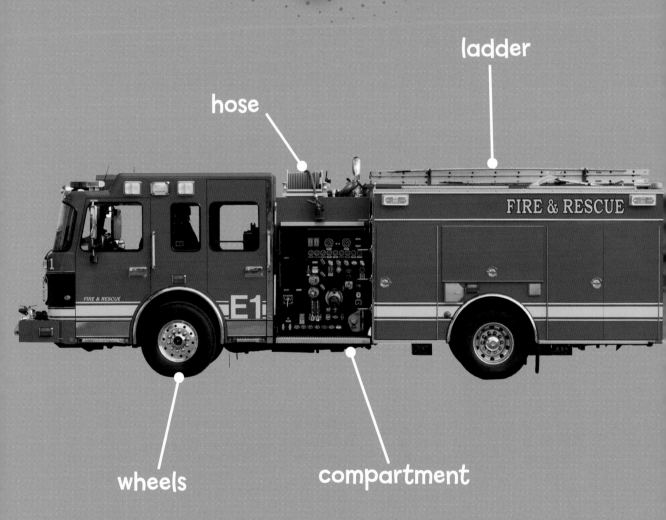

ladder

hose

wheels

compartment

Foam Fights Fire

Fire trucks don't just use water to fight fires. They also use foam. Foam is helpful for fighting fires caused by liquids that can catch fire easily. These kinds of fires can happen at airports. That's why many airports have special fire trucks. Fire trucks use foam to put out a fire by cutting off its oxygen. Oxygen helps fire grow.

Glossary

crankshaft: a long metal piece that connects a vehicle's engine to its wheels and helps them turn

diesel: a type of fuel and an engine powered by this fuel

ignite: to set on fire

nozzle: a short tube put on the end of a hose that controls the way water or foam flows out

oxygen tank: a container with oxygen inside, used for helping people breathe

piston: a rod that moves and changes energy into motion

valve: a device that controls the flow of liquid by opening and closing

Learn More

Besel, Jennifer M. *Fire Trucks*. Mankato, MN: Black Rabbit Books, 2023.

Britannica Kids: Firefighter
https://kids.britannica.com/kids/article/firefighter/624512

Kaiser, Brianna. *Look Inside a Bulldozer: How It Works*. Minneapolis: Lerner Publications, 2024.

Kiddle: Fire Engine Facts for Kids
https://kids.kiddle.co/Fire_engine

KidsHealth: What to Do in a Fire
https://kidshealth.org/en/kids/fire-safety.html

Nagle, Frances. *Fire Trucks to the Rescue!* New York: Gareth Stevens, 2023.

Index

Photo Acknowledgments

Image credits: 1000 Words/Shutterstock, p. 4; Robert Wilder Jr/Shutterstock, p. 5; Matthew Strauss/Shutterstock, p. 6; Stockbyte/Getty Images, p. 7; Philip Arno Photography/Shutterstock, p. 8; Renata Tyburczy/Alamy, p. 9; Paul Starosta/Getty Images, p. 10; Bill Oxford/Getty Images, p. 11; iliart/Shutterstock, p. 12; Krasowit/Shutterstock, p. 13; Bim/Getty Images, p. 14; Joe_Potato/Getty Images, p. 15; CBCK-Christine/Getty Images, p. 16; ChiccoDodiFC/Getty Images, p. 17; Pavel Gulea/Shutterstock, p. 18; narin phapnam/Shutterstock, p. 19; VCNW/Getty Images, p. 20.

Front cover: ryasick/Getty Images.